Quick & Easy
Way To Learn Japanese

Vinayak

Qualis Books

G T BOOK
AGENCY

ISBN : 81-87838-05-1
ISBN : 9788187838050

1st Published 2012
2nd Published 2015
3rd Published 2023
Reprinted 2025

Quick & Easy Way to Learn Japanese

Published by
Qualis Books
140, Medha Apartment
Mayur Vihar, Ext. Phase 1,
New Delhi - 110091
E-mail : qualisbooks@yahoo.co.in

Printed in India at
D.K. Fine Art Press
New Delhi.

Quick & Easy Way to Learn Japanese

Japanese language is considered to be one of the most difficult language to learn. However, the speaking part is not as difficult as the reading/writing is. As the title itself suggests, this book is aimed at students, backpackers or people who have only a passive interest in Japan or Japanese culture. As a result, the vocabulary/grammar is mainly confined to words, sentences that are used in daily life (shopping, traveling, public services etc.)

The grammar in Japanese language is fairly simple. The grammer is limited to basic sentence construction, parts of speech etc.

A table listing the Japanese language characters (hiragana and katakana) has been provided, however one word of caution, it takes a very long time to master the art of writing Japanese. In addition to the basic scripts there are Kanjis, which cannot be listed here (mainly because of their large number). Most of the book follows the romanization method, i.e writing the Japanese pronunciation in Roman alphabet.

This book can serve as a tool that will further deepen the curiosity of the reader towards this enigmatic yet beautiful country.

GAMBATTE!

CONTENTS

Part-3 (Practical Japanese)	146-178

At the post office, On the telephone, At the hotel, At market/public places, Announcements, Signs (airport,city), Small talk, Socialising, Local talk, At the bank, Doing business, Eating out, Emergency (police/doctor/hospital), Well wishing

PRONUNCIATION

Japanese pronunciation is not considered difficult for Hindi/ English language speakers. Unlike some other Asian languages (Chinese), it has no tones and most of its sounds are found in Hindi/english.

Vowel sounds

Vowels in Japanese can be either short or long. The long ones should be held twice as long as the short ones and are represented throughout this book with *a horizontal line on top of them.*

Table 1

Symbol	English	Japanese example
a	can't	ga-ka
ā	rather	sak-kā
i	sit	ki-ji
ī	see	shī-tsu
u	put	mu-ra
ū	soon	kū-ki
e	bed	I-ke
ē	reign	pē-ji
o	hot	chot-to
ō	saw	pas-pō-to

It is most important to pay attention to the long sounds because a slight change can alter the meaning completely. For ex.

Ka-re	he
Ka-rē	curry
o-ji-san	uncle
o-jī-san	grandfather
ningyo	mermaid
ningyō	doll

All vowels in the table above are 'pure' meaning they are pronounced individually. They should be pronounced clearly and slowly to make your self understood. For ex.

i-e (house), ī-e (no)

The vowel 'u' is sometimes not pronounced in Japanese. This 'silent' or 'reduced' vowel most often occurs between k and s and in verb endings like des and –mas.
Ex.- a-ri-ma-su is pronounced as a-ri-mas
De-su is pronounced as de-s

Consonant Sounds

Most consonant sounds are pretty close to the English ones. However, care needs to be taken for distinguishing between single and double consonants as this can produce a difference in meanings. Ex:

Saka is 'slope' and sakka is 'writer', similarly
Kako is 'past' and kakko is 'brackets'

The double consonants should be pronounced with a slight pause between them.

Table 2

Symbol	English	Japanese example
,b	big	ba-sho
ch	chill	chi-zu
d	them	dai-ga-ku
f	fun (almost like 'fw' with lips in rounded position)	fu-man
g	go (hard sound)	ga-man
h	hip	hi-to
j	jam	jum-bi
k	kick	kan-ji
m	man	mu-su-ko
n	no	no-ri
p	pick	pa-n
r	run (mix of 'l' and 'r')	re-mo-n
s	so	sa-ba-ku
sh	show	shi-ma
t	tip	ta-bi

ts	bits	tsu-na-mi
w	win	wa-ta
y	yes	yu-ki
z	is/zoo	zu-bo-n

Syllables are mostly pronounced evenly in Japanese, so there are no stressed syllables indicated anywhere in this book.

Also, for the double consonant sounds in Japanese language, the following are the corresponding pronunciation in English (indicated in bold type font).

JAPANESE	ENGLISH
Secchaku	Chernobyl
shusseki	Miss
Tappuri	Happy
Yukkuri	Kick

FREQUENT PRONUNCIATION MISTAKES IN JAPANESE

Mispronunciation is a part of foreign language learning. However, in case of Japanese this problem is compounded by the fact that there are often very slight changes in sounds which can alter the meaning completely. One has to be especially careful in getting his/her long sounds right as any mistake might convey a different meaning altogether and perhaps ruin the conversation. Let us look at some such words.

Word		often wrongly pronounced as
1. oishī (tasty)	-	ushi (cow)
2. kawaī (cute)	-	kowai(scary)
3. kare (he)	-	karē (curry)
4. kudasai (please)	-	kusai (stinky)
5. okashi (sweets)	-	okashī (weird,strange)
6 battā (butter)	-	batta (locust)
7. Hachimaki (headband)	-	Harumaki (spring rolls)
8. chizu (map)	-	chīzu (cheese)
9. biru (building)	-	bīru (beer)
10. byōin (hospital)	-	biyōin (beauty parlor)

A. JAPANESE LANGUAGE (READING & WRITING)

The Japanese did not have a developed writing system till about the 8th century A.D. when KANJI (Chinese characters) was declared as the official writing system of Japan. Kanji are pictorial ideographs and not a phonetic script. The complex characters that indicate an idea/concept are assigned readings in Japanese language and are very difficult to master. Most of the Kanji have multiple readings and complex stroke order. However, later on a unique Japanese writing system was developed as the Chinese characters were considered way to difficult to learn or write. This is the system of HIRAGANA and KATAKANA scripts (see table). HIRAGANA is mainly used to write native Japanese words and KATAKANA on the other hand is used for writing words of foreign origin. The basic vocabulary of Japanese, of which Chinese loanwords are an integral part, is written in a mixture of kanji and hiragana.

1-KANJI:

Kanji are ideographs (symbols that each represent a concept, idea or thing as well as pronunciation rather than a word or set of words) borrowed athe Chinese language. Ex.本 (hon) for 'book', 日本語 (nihongo) for 'Japanese language', 息子 (musuko) for 'son'. Kanji can be made up of anything from one to over 20 brush strokes written in a particular order. A lot of Kanji characters have two or more ways of being pronounced depending on the context. For ex. The kanjii 水 is pronounced 'mizu' when it means 'water', but 'sui' when it's part of another word like 水牛 (pronounced suigyuu) for 'water buffalo'.

There are over 2,000 kanji in use in modern Japanese, of which 1945 are considered essential for everyday use. Among these, the ministry of education has designated 1006 characters as basic, which are taught at primary school level.

2-HIRAGANA

Hiragana is used to represent particles and grammatical endings particular to Japanese and is placed alongside the ideographic characters. One single Japanese word can contain both scripts. There are 46 basic hiragana characters each representing a particular syllable. They can be combined to represent over 100 different syllables (see table)

銀行はどこですか *ginkō -wa doko des ka* (Where is the bank?)

In this phrase the word for 'bank' (ginkou) is written in kanji (銀行), but the rest (the particle wa (は), the question word doko (どこ), the verb des (です) and the interrogative particle ka (か) in hiragana.

3-KATAKANA

Each hiragana character also has a katakana equivalent (see table). Katakana is used to represent loanwords from other languages, mostly from English. They are also used to write foreign names. Foreign travelers might want to figure out how to write their names in Japanese (using katakana).

クレジットカード	*kurejitto kādo*	credit card
私の名前はニシャです。	*watashi no namae wa nisha des.*	My name is Nisha
インドから来ました。	*Indo kara kimashita*	I am from India

The Japanese words for 'credit card', 'Nisha' and 'India'are all written in katakana.The tables given on the next page (below) show the basic as well as some of the combined hiragana and katakana characters. For each vowel & syllable the pronunciation is given in red with it's hiragana symbol above and katakana symbol below it.

Table 3
Hiragana and Katakana script table

あ	い	う	え	お								
a	i	u	e	o								
ア	イ	ウ	エ	オ								
か	き	く	け	こ	きゃ	きゅ	きょ	が	ぎ	ぐ	げ	ご
ka	ki	ku	ke	ko	kya	kyu	kyo	ga	gi	gu	ge	go
カ	キ	ク	ケ	コ	キャ	キュ	キョ	ガ	ギ	グ	ゲ	ゴ
さ	し	す	せ	そ	しゃ	しゅ	しょ	ざ	じ	ず	ぜ	ぞ
sa	shi	su	se	so	sha	shu	sho	za	ji	zu	ze	zo
サ	シ	ス	セ	ソ	シャ	シュ	ショ	ザ	ジ	ズ	ゼ	ソ
た	ち	つ	て	と	ちゃ	ちゅ	ちょ	だ	ぢ	づ	で	ど
ta	chi	tsu	te	to	cha	chu	cho	da	ji	zu	de	do
タ	チ	ツ	テ	ト	チャ	チュ	チョ	ダ	ヂ	ヅ	デ	ド
な	に	ぬ	ね	の	にゃ	にゅ	にょ					
na	ni	nu	ne	no	nya	nyu	nyo					
ナ	ニ	ヌ	ネ	ノ	ニャ	ニュ	ニョ					
は	ひ	ふ	へ	ほ	ひゃ	ひゅ	ひょ	ば	び	ぶ	べ	ぼ
ha	hi	fu	he	ho	hya	hyu	hyo	ba	bi	bu	be	bo
ハ	ヒ	フ	ヘ	ホ	ヒャ	ヒュ	ヒョ	バ	ビ	ブ	ベ	ボ

ま み む め も みゃ みゅ みょ ぱ ぴ ぷ ぺ ぽ

ma mi mu me mo mya myu myo pa pi pu pe po

マ ミ ム メ モ ミャ ミュ ミョ パ ピ プ ペ ポ

や ゆ よ

ya yu yo

ヤ ユ ヨ

ら り る れ ろ りゃ りゅ りょ

ra ri ru re ro rya ryu ryo

ラ リ ル レ ロ リャ リュ リョ

わ を ぎゃ ぎゅ ぎょ びゃ びゅ びょ

wa o gya gyu gyo bya byu byo

ワ ヲ ギャ ギュ ギョ ビャ ビュ ビョ

ん じゃ じゅ じょ ぴゃ ぴゅ ぴょ

n ja ju jo pya pyu pyo

ン ジャ ジュ ジョ ピャ ピュ ピョ

BASIC GRAMMAR

Below I have discussed the essential Japanese grammar required for, to put it simply, getting your message across in a Japanese environment. I personally feel that with a few appropriate words, the right gestures and some basic grasp of the grammar, life can be smooth in any alien environment for the casual traveler.

For the sake of convenience, I have added the topics in alphabetical order.

ARTICLES

Japanese does not have words equivalent to the English indefinite/definite articles like 'a' 'an', 'the'. Ex.

It is a car *Kuruma des*

It is the hotel *Hoteru des*

Words are used without the articles and one has to guess from the context which article is meant. In order to point out to a specific item (the), one has to use a demonstrative.

ADJECTIVES

As in English/hindi, adjectives come before the noun they describe. There are two type of adjectives in the Japanese language. ,i adjectives (that end in the vowel sound 'i') and 'na adjectives'(that end in 'na' sound).

That is an expensive restaurant - *are wa takai restoran des*('i' type)

Tomoko is a pretty girl - *tomoko wa kirei-na josei des.* ('na' type)

List of basic adjectives

Adjectives	English
Tanosh-ī	pleasant
uresh-ī	happy
kanash-ī	sad
yasash-ī	kind/simple/easy
naga-i	long
mijika-i	short
tō-i	far
chika-i	close/near
haya-i	quick
nemu-i	tired

genki-na	healthy/feeling fine
ski-na	like
yūmei-na	famous
shizuka-na	silent/quiet
Taka-i	expensive/tall
yasu-i	cheap
atsu-i	hot thing(oven, hot water,fever)
atsu-i	hot (weather)
tsumeta-i	cold (to the touch)
samu-i	cold (weather)
ī	good
waru-i	bad
ōkī	big
chīsa-i	small
atarash-ī	new
furu-i	old
isogash-ī	busy
oish-ī	delicious
omoshiro-i	interesting
muzukash-ī	hard (difficult)

ADVERBS

Adverbs, which describe a verb or an adjective, can be formed by replacing the 'i' ending of the ' -i adjectives' with –ku. For example, the adjective hayai (fast), becomes the adverb hayaku.

However, there are many adverbs in Japanese that exist as a word. For example, totemo (very), yukkuri (slowly) etc.

Be (existence)

The word des corresponds to the English verb 'be'. However, like any verb of the Japanese language, it does not change according to who or what it refers to; des can mean 'I am' or 'she is' according to the situation. There is only one form for all subjects. Japanese verbs change forms when expressing the past tense or negative.

Present positive	**Present negative**
Des	dewa arimasen
Past positive	**past negative**
Desh-ta	dewa arimasen desh-ta

I am Indian

Watashi-wa indo jin des

I am not a doctor

Watashi-wa isha dewa arimasen

It was rainy yesterday

Kinō-wa ame desh-ta

The person I met last night was not Mr. Tanaka

Yūbe atta hito wa tanaka san dewa arimasen deshta

FUTURE TENSE

There is no future tense in Japanese language. It is expressed using the same forms as for the present tense. One has to guess from the context as to what time frame is being taken into account. In order to make one's sentences (tense) clear one can use a word or expression of time such as 'ashta' (tomorrow), rai-getsu (next month).

KEIGO (POLITE LANGUAGE)

Keigo is usually the most difficult to grasp for foreigners in japan. The Japanese people pay special attention to a person's seniority during interaction. Consequently, the kind of words/ expressions that one would generally use with his/her colleague change completely.It is not possible to go into a detailed discussion of KEIGO in this book but below are some of the things/precautions that would make life a lot easier for a foreigner in Japan. The most commonly used polite form is the –mas form of the verbs. All foreigners are expected to interact with Japanese people using the –mas form of verbs. For example, tabemas (to eat), aimas(to meet), mimas(to see) and so on.

Also, the Japanese people frequently use the prefix o- and go- to indicate respect/reverence towards a particular concept/ thing/person. Example,

Sake (Japanese drink) becomes o-sake

Rice/meal becomes go-han

Shu-jin (husband) changes to go-shujin (somebody else's honorable husband)

***Never** use shujin for somebody else's husband.

* Also never use the prefix o- and go- for yourself or your own things.

*Avoid the use of second person pronouns, as they are too direct and impolite.

*Always address a Japanese person by adding '-san' at the end of his name. For example, Tanaka-san, tomoko-san etc.

Below are some words with their KEIGO (polite) forms. Bear in mind that there are humble forms for same words as well. It is not possible to go into a detailed discussion about them in this book. People really interested can refer to a number of web sites that explain the polite language and expressions of Japan.

Verb (normal polite form)	Verb (more polite/with seniors)
mimas (to see)	go-ran
ikimas (to go)	irassharu
shimas (to do)	nasaru
tabemas (to eat)	meshi agaru

NEGATIVE

To make a verb in the present tense negative, replace the ending –mas with –masen

I drink	- watashi-wa nomimas
I don't drink	watashi-wa nomimasen
I eat	- watashi-wa tabemas
I don't eat	watashi-wa tabemasen

To make a verb in the past tense negative, replace –mashta with –masen deshta

I came by bus	watashi-wa basu de kimashta (past positive)

I did not come by bus	watashi-wa basu de kimasen deshta (past negative)

In Japanese, the adjectives too have a negative form. For 'i' adjectives replace the ending 'i' with –ku and negate by adding 'arimasen' or 'nai des'

Atarashi-i	- atarashi-kunai des (not new)
Furu-i	- furu-kunai des (not old)

For 'na' adjectives, drop the 'na' ending and add (or negate them) by adding –dewa arimasen:

Kirei-na	- kirei dewa-arimasen (not beautiful/pretty)
Shinsetsu-na	- shinsetsu dewa-arimasen (not kind)

NOUNS

Japanese language has no gender (masculine or feminine) or plural forms. One has to always use the same form of the noun, irrespective of whether you are referring to a masculine or feminine person, object, place etc, and whether it is singular or plural.

Box/boxes - hako

Person/people - hito

Ticket/tickets - kippu

There is the suffix –tachi that can be added to word ending for 'we' or 'us' and 'them'

We/us - watashi-tachi

Them - sono hito-tachi

In a phrase, nouns are always followed by a particle (see **particles**)

PARTICLES

A Japanese noun/pronoun is generally followed by a particle. Particles are short words that display the function of the preceding word in that particular sentence. They can show the subject (who/what is doing something) or the object (the person/thing that is affected by the action) of the sentence. Sometimes the particles can also behave as prepositions like the 'in' and 'to' of English. Let us discuss some of the most commonly used particles in everyday language.

1.**Ga** – subject particle

This particle simply indicates the subject of the sentence

This is my house

Kore ga watashi-no ie des

2.**Wa** –topic particle

This particle marks the topic or focal point of the sentence. It is often used when clarifying or stressing a particular point.

Watashi-wa indo-jin des

I am an Indian

3. O - object particle

This particle marks the object of the sentence

I drink beer

Watashi-wa (subject) *bīru* (object) *o nomimas* (verb) - I drink beer

Watashi-wa (subject) *gohan* (object) *o tabemas* (verb) - I eat food (rice)

4. **no** –possessive particle (**also see possessive case below**)

this particle indicates that something belongs to someone/ something.

Watashi-no hon	- my book
Anata-no pen	- your pen

5. **ni** –particle for time/location/destination

nichi yōbi ni	- On Sunday (time)
san ji ni	- At three o clock (time)
heya ni	- In the room (location)
eki ni	- to the station (destination)

6. **e** particle (direction)

the particle 'e' indicates only direction and is used mainly with 3 verbs – 'to come', 'to go', 'to return'. We can compare it with the destination function of 'ni' particle above.

Ginza e ikimas	- To go to ginza
Hoteru e kaerimas	- return to the hotel
Uchi ni/e kimas	- come to the house

7.**de** particle

The particle is similar to 'ni' particle in that it indicates location- with one big difference. 'ni' particle is only for location whereas in 'de' particle action at a particular location is emphasized upon.

Kissaten de kōhī o nomimas - I will drink coffee at the coffee shop

Depāto de kaimono o shimashta- I did shopping at the department store

8. **ka** (interrogative particle)

The particle ka is added at the end of a statement to turn it into a question.

Kore-wa nan des ka - What is this?

Hoteru-wa doko des ka - where is the hotel?

PAST

There are only two basic tenses in Japanese- present and past. The present tense is also used to express future. To form the past tense, replace the –mas ending with –mashta *shokuji o shimashta* - I had my meal

Bīru o nomimashta - I drank beer

Terebi o mimashta - I watched TV

As in present tense, the verbs do not change in the past tense too according to the subject.

POSSESSIVE CASE

The most common way of showing the possessive case is by using the particle 'no' after the noun, proper noun that indicates the possession.

My friend
Watashi-no tomodachi

My book
Watashi-no hon

This is my book
Kore-wa watashi-no hon des

Schoolteacher
gakkō no sensei

My house
Watashi-no ie

Her pen
Kanojo-no pen

The verb *motte-imas* (to have) or the expression ga arimas (there is something that I have) can also be used to express possession.

I have money
Watashi-wa okane o motte-imas

I have a car
Watashi-wa kuruma ga arimas

VOCABULARY

ENGLISH	JAPANESE
Above	ue ni
Across	yoko gitte
After	ato
At (time)	ni (see particles)
At (place)	de (see particles)
Before (time)	mae
During	aida
For (purpose)	tame
From	kara
In(place)	ni (see particles)
In (time)	naka
In front of	mae
Near	chikaku
Through	tō shte
Under	shita ni
With	issho ni
Without	snashi

PRONOUNS

Pronouns are often omitted in Japanese when the person is obvious from context. Japanese pronouns can vary as per the level of formality.

ENGLISH	JAPANESE
I / me	watashi (polite), watakushi (formal), boku/ore (used by men)
You	anata (polite), kimi (used by men for subordinates)
She/her	kanojo
He/him	kare
We/us	watashi-tachi
You (people)	anata-tachi
They/them	kare-ra, kanojo-tachi

There are no different pronouns for subjects (I, she), objects (me, her) and possessives (mine, her). The difference between these is indicated by a particle that follows the pronoun in the sentence. 'Wa' for object, 'o' for object and no for the possessive case. (see particles)

This is mine
Kore-wa watashino des

I saw her
Watashi-ga kanojo o mimashta

As mentioned in the KEIGO section above, it is common practice to avoid using second person pronouns, as this is considered too direct and rude sometimes.

QUESTIONS

To ask questions (yes/no), add 'ka' to the end of the sentence.

Is this the tourist office?
Kore-wa kankō-an-nai-jo des ka

Where is the station?
Eki-wa doko des ka

QUESTION WORDS

ENGLISH	JAPANESE
Who?	dare
What?	Nan/na-ni
Which?	dore
When?	itsu
Where?	doko
How?	Dono you ni
Why?	Naze

Who is it?

Dare desu ka

What is this?

Kore-wa nan des ka

What are you doing?

Nani o shite imas ka

When is the next bus?

Tsugi no basu-wa itsu des ka

At what time does the train leave?

Densha-wa nan-ji ni demas ka

Where are the restrooms?

Toire-wa doko des ka

How much does it cost?

Ikura des ka

How does this work?

Dono yō-ni shimas ka

Which train goes to Tokyo?

Dono densha-ga Tokyo ni ikimas ka

THIS/THAT (DEMONSTRATIVE)

The following words are used to point out a person or an object. Note that all these words follow the ko-, so-, a- pattern. Ko- refers to someone or something close to the speaker, so- to someone/something close to the listener and a- for something far from both the speaker and the listener.

Kore (this)	sore (that)	are (that over there)
Kono (this one)	sono (that one)	ano (that one over there)
Koko (here)	soko (there)	asoko (over there)
Kochira (this way)	sochira (that way)	achira (that way over there)

VERBS

Verbs are not very complex in Japanese language. They do not change according to the person. For example, the verb 'shimas' can mean 'I do', 'you do' both. Another thing is that Japanese has only two basic tenses, present and past. The present tense is also used to express the future.

Verbs in Japanese dictionary are listed in their plain forms. This plain form is not suited for conversations and instead the polite form, i.e the 'mas' form is used in this book. In the table below I have listed some important verbs in both mas and the plain forms, but I would strongly advise readers to memorize/use 'mas' form for their conversation.

Note: All Japanese verbs in plain form end with 'u' sound.

VERBS

'mas' form	'plain form
i-mas (to say)	iu
omoi-mas (to think)	omou
naraimas (to learn)	narau
yomimas (to read)	yomu
sumimas (to live)	sumu
yasumimas (to rest)	yasumu
erabimas (to select)	erabu
isogimas (to hurry)	isogu
hanashimas (to talk)	hanasu
kikimas (to hear)	kiku
ikimas (to go)	iku
hikimas (to pull)	hiku
demas (to go out)	deru
kimas (to wear)	kiru
nemas (to sleep)	neru
wasuremas (to forget)	wasureru
ochimas (to drop)	ochiru
hajimemas (to start)	hajimeru
agemas (to give)	ageru
wakarimas (to understand)	wakaru

nakimas (to cry)	naku
machimas (to wait)	matsu
mochimas (to hold)	motsu
arimas (to exist)	aru
hairimas (to enter)	hairu
shirimas (to know)	shiru
aimas (to meet)	au
hashirimas (to run)	hashiru
tabe-mas (to eat)	tabe-ru
shi-mas (to do)	su-ru
nomi-mas (to drink)	no-mu
kai-mas (to buy)	ka-u
iki-mas (to go)	I-ku
kaeri-mas (to return)	kae-ru
okimas (to get up)	oki-ru
kimas (to come)	ku-ru
mimas (to see)	mi-ru

WORD ORDER

The word order in Japanese is the same as in Hindi. Both follow SOV (subject, object, verb) pattern. Ex.

Watashi-wa(subject) mizu (object) o nomimas(verb) {I drink water}

However, in English the above order would change to SVO (subject, verb, object) pattern as can be seen in the sentence 'I drink water'. In Japanese the subject is sometimes omitted from the sentence if it is clear from the context.

I bought a ticket to Tokyo

(watashi-wa) tōkyō made no chiketto o kaimash-ta

When constructing Japanese sentences it is important to keep each particle right after the word it can be associated with. Nothing else can come between a word and it's particle. These building blocks of Japanese sentences can be moved around in a single sentence, so long as the basic SOV order (see above) is maintained. The verb always comes at the end of the sentence. Compare the following sentences

Watashi-wa restoran-de kōhī o nomimashta

Watashi-wa kōhī o restoran de nomimashta

Yes/No

Yes	-	hai
No	-	ī-e

Do you understand?

Wakarimashta ka

Yes, I do

Hai wakarimashta

No, I don't understand

ī-e wakarimasen

GREETINGS (AISATSU)

English	Japanese
Excuse me	sumimasen
Farewell	sayōnara
Good morning	ohayō Gozaimas
Good afternoon	konnichiwa
Good evening	konbanwa
Goodnight	oyasumi Nasai
Goodbye	sayōnara
Hello	konnichiwa
How are you?	ogenki des ka
I am fine	genki des
Mention not	dō-itashimashte
Okay	ok/ Wakarimashta
Sorry	gomen Nasai
Thank you	arigatō Gozaimasu
Welcome!	irasshai!

B. VOCABULARY

CARDINAL NUMBERS (SŪJI)

No.	English	Japanese
1.	One	ichi
2.	Two	ni
3.	Three	san
4.	Four	shi (Yon)
5.	Five	go
6.	Six	roku
7.	Seven	shichi (Nana)
8.	Eight	hachi
9.	Nine	kyū
10.	Ten	jyū
11.	Eleven	jyū -ichi
12.	Twelve	jyū -ni
13.	Thirteen	jyū -san
14.	Fourteen	jyū-yon
15.	Fifteen	jyū -go

16.	Sixteen	jyū -roku
17.	Seventeen	jyū -shichi
18.	Eighteen	jyū-hachi
19.	Nineteen	jyū -kyuu
20.	Twenty	ni-jyū
21.	Twenty one	ni-jyū ichi
22.	Twenty two	ni-jyū ni
23	Twenty three	ni-jyū san
24.	Twenty four	ni-jyū yon
25.	Twenty five	ni-jyū go
26.	Twenty six	ni-jyū roku
27.	Twenty seven	ni-jyū shichi
28.	Twenty eight	ni-jyū hachi
29.	Twenty nine	ni-jyū kyū
30.	Thirty	san-jyū
31.	Thirty one	san-jyū ichi
32.	Thirty two	san-jyū ni
33.	Thirty three	san-jyū san
34.	Thirty four	san-jyū yon

35.	Thirty five	san-jyū go
36.	Thirty six	san-jyū roku
37.	Thirty seven	san-jyū shichi
38.	Thirty eight	san-jyū hachi
39.	Thirty nine	san-jyū kyū
40.	Forty	yon-jyū
41.	Forty one	yon-jyū ichi
42.	Forty two	yon-jyū ni
43.	Forty three	yon-jyū san
44.	Forty four	yon-jyū yon
45.	Forty five	yon-jyū go
46.	Forty six	yon-jyū roku
47.	Forty seven	yon-jyū shichi
48.	Forty eight	yon-jyū hachi
49.	Forty nine	yon-jyū kyū
50.	Fifty	go-jyū
51.	Fifty one	go-jyū ichi
52.	Fifty two	go-jyū ni
53.	Fifty three	go-jyū san

54.	Fifty four	go-jyū yon
55.	Fifty five	go-jyū go
56.	Fifty six	go-jyū roku
57.	Fifty seven	go-jyū shichi
58.	Fifty eight	go-jyū hachi
59.	Fifty nine	go-jyū kyū
60.	Sixty	roku-jyū
61.	Sixty one	roku-jyū ichi
62.	Sixty two	roku-jyū ni
63.	Sixty three	roku-jyū san
64.	Sixty four	roku-jyū yon
65.	Sixty five	roku-jyū go
66.	Sixty six	roku-jyū roku
67.	Sixty seven	roku-jyū shichi
68.	Sixty eight	roku-jyū hachi
69.	Sixty nine	roku-jyū kyū
70.	Seventy	nana-jyū
71.	Seventy one	nana-jyū ichi
72.	Seventy two	nana-jyū ni

73.	Seventy three	nana-jyū san
74.	Seventy four	nana-jyū yon
75.	Seventy five	nana-jyū go
76.	Seventy six	nana-jyū roku
77.	Seventy seven	nana-jyū shichi
78.	Seventy eight	nana-jyū hachi
79.	Seventy nine	nana-jyū kyū
80.	Eighty	hachi-jyū
81.	Eighty one	hachi-jyū ichi
82.	Eighty two	hachi-jyū ni
83.	Eighty three	hachi-jyū san
84.	Eighty four	hachi-jyū yon
85.	Eighty five	hachi-jyū go
86.	Eighty six	hachi-jyū roku
87.	Eighty seven	hachi-jyū shichi
88.	Eighty eight	hachi-jyū hachi
89.	Eighty nine	hachi-jyū kyū
90.	Ninety	kyū-jyū
91.	Ninety one	kyū-jyū ichi

92.	Ninety two	kyū-jyū ni
93.	Ninety three	kyū-jyū san
94.	Ninety four	kyū-jyū yon
95.	Ninety five	kyū-jyū go
96.	Ninety six	kyū-jyū roku
97.	Ninety seven	kyū-jyū shichi
98.	Ninety eight	kyū-jyū hachi
99.	Ninety nine	kyū-jyū kyū
100.	One hundred	hyaku
500.	Five hundred	go-hyaku
1000.	One thousand	sen
5,000	Five thousand	go-sen
10,000.	Ten thousand	(ichi) man
100,000	Hundred thousand	jyū man
1,000,000	One million	hyaku man

ORDINAL NUMBERS

To use an ordinal number in Japanese, just add –ban to the end of the corresponding cardinal number.

1st	I-chi-ban
2nd	ni-ban
3rd	sam-ban
4th	yom-ban
5th	go-ban

A quarter	yom-bun no I-chi
A third	sam-bun no ichi
A half	ham-bun
Three quarters	yom-bun no san
All	Zem-bu
None	na-shi
Add	tasu
Divide	waru
Multiply	kakeru
Subtract	hiku
Money	okane
Yen	en (Japanese currency)
Dollar	doru
Rupee	rupī
Euro	yūro

COUNTERS

In Japanese, when expressing a certain number of objects, people or animals, the cardinal number is followed by a counter. Counters, also commonly known as 'classifiers', indicate the size, shape and function of things and distinguish between objects, people and animals. There are two types of counters, generic and specific counters. The generic counters can be used to count most objects except for people or animals.

No.	Pronunciation
1.	hi-to-tsu
2.	fu-ta-tsu
3.	mittsu
4.	yottsu
5.	I-tsu-tsu
6.	muttsu
7.	nanatsu
8.	yattsu
9.	kokonotsu
10.	tō
for numbers higher than 10	...ko

Except for the last generic counter, there is no need to add the cardinal number before the counter as this already makes part of the counter.

Ex. *Mikan o futatsu kudasai* (Please give me 2 oranges)
Below is a list of some basic specific counters used in daily life.

Age	..sai
Animals	..hiki/piki/biki
Books	..satsu
Bottles,pens (long, cylindrical objects)	..hon/bon/pon
floors (building)	..kai
people	..nin
sheets	..mai
time	..ji
vehicles	..dai

WEIGHTS AND MEASURES (SOKTEI)

English	Japanese
Balance	hakari
Dozen	dāsu
Foot	fīto
Gram	guramu
Inch	inchi
Kilogram	kiroguramu
Litre	rittoru
Metre	mētoru
Mile	mairu
Ounce	onsu
Pound	pondo
Yard	yādo

TIME (JIKAN)

English	Japanese
Afternoon	gogo
A quarter of an hour	jyū-gofun mae
Anniversary	kinenbi
At times	tama ni
Century	seiki
Dawn	yo ake
Day before yesterday	ototoi
Day after tomorrow	asatte
Day-to-day	hi-bi no
Decade	jyū nenkan
Evening	yūgata
Fortnight	ni shyūkan
Golden jubilee	gojyū nen -kinenbi
Hour	-kan
Last night	yūbe
Last time	zenkai

Late	osoi
Leap year	uru-udoshi
Morning	asa
Midnight	shinya
Minute	-fun, -bun, -pun
New-year	shin nen
Nowadays	kono goro
Period	kikan
Second	byō
Sometimes	toki doki
The year before	kyonen
Time	jikan
Today	kyō
Tomorrow	ashita
Yesterday	kinō

DAYS OF THE WEEK (SHYŪ)

English	Japanese
Monday	getsu-yōbi
Tuesday	ka-yōbi
Wednesday	sui-yōbi
Thursday	moku-yōbi
Friday	kin-yōbi
Saturday	do-yōbi
Sunday	nichi-yōbi

MONTHS (GATSU)

English	Japanese
January	ichi-gatsu
February	ni-gatsu
March	san-gatsu
April	shi-gatsu
May	go-gatsu
June	roku-gatsu
July	shichi-gatsu
August	hachi-gatsu
September	ku-gatsu
October	jyū-gatsu
November	jyūichi-gatsu
December	jyūni-gatsu

What time is it now?
Ima nan-ji des ka

It is half past 10
Ima jyū-ji han des

It is quarter to 6
Ima roku-ji jy ūgofun mae des

I will go next month
Watashi wa raigetsu ikimas

What is the date today? What day is it today?
Kyō wa nan-nichi des ka/ kyō wa nani-yōbi des ka

On the 10th of this month/next month
Kon-getsu/raigetsu no tōka

Today is friday
Kyōwa kinyōbi des

Tomorrow is saturday
Ashta wa doyōbi des

MONEY & CURRENCY EXCHANGE (OKANE TO RYŌGAE)

The currency of japan is yen. One should always carry sufficient cash with him/her when in japan. The reason being that a lot of people still prefer cash to credit card in Japan.

English	Japanese
Bank	ginkō
Cash	genkin
Change money	ryōgae
Charge	ryōkin
Cheque	kogitte
Coin	koin
Credit card	kurejitto kādo
Currency	kahei
Currency note	shihei
Debit card	debitto kādo
Dollar	doru
Dollar rate	doru rēto
Foreign exchange	gaikoku kawase
Free	tada

Exchange rate	kōkan rēto
Receipt	reshīto
Refund	harai modoshi
Traveller's cheque	toraberāzu chekku
Withdraw (money)	hikidashi

HUMAN BODY (KARADA)

English	Japanese
Ankle	ashikubi
Arm	ude
Armpit	waki no shita
Back	senaka
Beard	hige
Belly	onaka
Blood	chi
Body	karada
Bosom	mune
Brain	nō
Breast	chibusa
Cheek	hoppeta
Chest	mune
Chin	shita ago
Ear	mimi
Elbow	hiji

Eye	me
Eyeball	me-dama
Eyebrow	mayu
Eyelash	matsuge
Eyelid	mabuta
Face	kao
Finger	yubi
Fist	kobushi
Flesh	nikutai
Foot	ashi
Gum	shiniku
Hand	te
Hair	ke
Head	atama
Heart	kokoro, shinzô
Heel	kakato
Hip	shiri
Jaw	ago
Knee	hiza

Kidney	jinzō
Leg	ashi
Lip	kuchibiru
Liver	kanzō
Lung	haizō
Moustache	kuchihige
Mouth	kuchi
Nail	tsume
Neck	kubi
Nose	hana
Palm	te no hira
Shoulder	kata
Skin	hada
Skull	zugai-kotsu
Spine	sebone
Sole	ashi no ura
Stomach	hara
Tooth	ha
Thigh	mata

Throat	nodo
Thumb	oya yubi
Vein	jyōmyaku
Waist	koshi
Wrist	tekubi

FOOD & HEALTH
FOODSTUFF (SHOKUHIN)

English	Japanese
Appetite	shokuyoku
Appetizer	apetaizā
Apple pie	appuru pai
Beansprouts	moyashi
Beanstalk	mame no kuki
Beef	gyūniku
Boiled egg	yude tamago
Bread	pan
Breakfast	asagohan
Buffet lunch	serufu sābisu/ chyūshoku
Buffet meal	serufu sābisu
Biscuit	hotto bisuketto
Butter	battā
Cake	kēki
Candy	kyandē

Cheddar	chedā
Cheese	chīzu
Cheeseburger	chīzu bāgā
Cheesecake	chīzu kēki
Chicken	chikin
Chili sauce	chiri Sōsu
Corn	tōmorokoshi
Cornflakes	kōn furēkusu
Cottage cheese	kotēji chīzu
Curd	gyō-nyū
Curry	karē
Custard	kasutādo
Dessert	dezāto
Diet	dai-etto
Dinner	yūshoku
Dish	ryōri
Drumstick	doramu schikku
Egg	tamago
Egg white	shiromi

Egg yolk	kimi
Fish	sakana
Flour	komugiko
French fries	furaido poteto
French toast	furenchi tōsto
Fried egg	furaido eggu
Fritter	furittā
Fruit-cake	furūtsu kēki
Fruit-salad	furūtsu sarada
Green salad	gurīn sarada
Hamburger	hambāgā
Honey	hachimitsu
Hotdog	hotto doggu
Ice	kōri
Ice cream	aisu kurīmu
Jam	jamu
Jelly	zerī
Junk food	janku fūdo
Kebab	kebabu

Lamb meat	ko-hitsuji niku
Lamb chop	ramu choppu
Lentil	renzu mame
Lunch	hiru gohan
Macaroni	makaroni
Main course	me-in Ryōri
Margarine	māgarin
Mayonnaise	mayonēzu
Meal	shokuji
Meat	niku
Mutton	maton
Noodles	nūdoru
Nougat	nuga
Oatmeal	ōto mīru
Oil	abura
Olive oil	oribu-yu
Omelette	omuretsu
Pasta	pasuta
Pastries	pēsutorī

Pepperoni	paparōni
Pickle	pikurusu
Pizza	piza
Pork	buta niku
Pulse	mame
Rice	kome, Gohan
Rice pudding	raisu pudingu
Salad	sarada
Salad dressing	sarada doresshingu
Salmon	sake
Salt	shio
Sandwich	sandoicchi
Sardine	sādin, iwashi
Sauce	sōsu
Sausage	sōsēji
Seafood	kaisan Shokuhin
Sesam	goma
Snack	oyatsu
Soup	sūpu

Soyabean	daizu
Soya sauce	shōyu
Spaghetti	spagetti
Sprout	shin-me
Stock	dashi
Sugar	satō
Sweetener	kanmiryō
Sweets	okashi
Syrup	shiroppu
Tartar sauce	tarutaru Sōsu
Toasted bread	tōsto
Tomato ketchup	tomato kechappu
Tomato puree	tomato pyūre
Tomato sauce	tomato sōsu
Vegetable soup	yasai sūpu
Venison	shika no Niku
Vinegar	su
Wafer	vēhāsu
White meat	shiromi no niku

BEVERAGES (NOMIMONO)

English	Japanese
Apple juice	appuru Jūsu
Beer	bīru
Black coffee	burakku kō hi
Brandy	burandē
Buttermilk	batā Miruku
Cappuccino	kapuchino
Champagne	sham-pan
Coffee	kō hi
Cognac	konyakku
Decaffeinated	kafein nuki
Draft beer	nama bīru
Espresso coffee	esupuresso kō hi
Gin	jin
Juice	jū su
Lemonade	remon-sui
Lemon tea	remon tē

Liquor	rikā
Malt liquor	bakuga-shu
Malt whisky	moruto whiskī
Milk	miruku, gyūnyū
Milkshake	miruku sēki
Mineral water	mineraru wōta
Red wine	aka wain
Rum	ramu-shu
Sake	sake (Japanese alcoholic drink)
Spirits	jōryū-shu
Tea	ocha
Tequila	tekīra
Vodka	votsuka
Whisky	uisuki
White wine	waito wain
Wine	wain

VEGETABLES (YASAI)

English	Japanese
Aubergine	nasu
Beans	mame
Carrot	ninjin
Cauliflower	karifurawā
Cabbage	kyabetsu
Coriander	koriandā
Cucumber	kyūri
Garlic	nin-niku
Ginger	shōga
Lemon	remon
Mint	hakka
Okra	okura
Onion	tamanegi
Peas	endō

Pepper	koshō
Potato	jagaimo
Pumpkin	kabocha
Radish	radesshu
Spinach	hōrensō
Tomato	tomato
Turnip	kabu

FRUITS (KUDAMONO)

English	Japanese
Almond	āmondo
Apple	ringo
Apricot	anzu
Banana	banana
Blackberry	kuro-ichigo
Chestnut	kuri
Coconut	yashi no mi
Custard	kasutādo
Date	yashi
Fig	ichijiku
Guava	guaba
Groundnut	pinatsu
Mango	mango
Orange	orenji
Papaya	papaiya
Pear	nashi

Pineapple	painappuru
Pistachio	pistachio
Pomegranate	zakuro
Raisin	rezun
Sugarcane	satō kibi
Sweetpotato	satsuma imo
Tamarind	tamarindo
Watermelon	suika

SPICES (SUPAISU)

English	Japanese
Alum	myōban
Aniseed	anisu no mi
Blackpepper	kuro-koshō
Camphor	shōnō
Cardamom	karudamon
Chilli	tōgarashi
Cinnamon	shinamon
Clove	chōji
Cumin seed	kumin shīdo
Mace	mesu
Mint	minto
Musk	jakō
Mustard	karashi
Nutmeg	natsumegu
Oregano	oregano
Parsley	paseri
Saffron	safuran
Turmeric	ukon
White pepper	shiro koshō

Grains

English	Japanese
Kidney beans	ingen mame
Lentil	renzu mame
Millet	kibi
Oat	ōtomugi
Sesame	goma
Wheat	mugi
A pinch of	tsumami
A dash of	shōryō
A handful of	wazuka
Calories	karori
Canned foods	kanzume Shokuhin
Cuisine	ryōri
Deep fry	tappuri ageru
Diet	daietto
Fried	itameta
Helping	okawari

I am full	ippai!
Nutritious	eiyō no aru
Preservative	bōfuzai
Roasted	yaki
Season	aji-zukeru
Seasoning	chōmiryō
Smoked	ibushita
Sour	suppai
Spicy	karai
Sweet	amai
Salty	shoppai
Taste	aji
Tasteless	mazui

JAPANESE CUISINE

Below are the names of some popular Japanese dishes. It is not possible to have a comprehensive list so the list contains some common/popular dishes. A note for the vegetarians- almost all of Japanese cuisine has meat/fish in some form or the other. So it is very difficult to have a purely vegetarian meal!

ama ebi	sweet prawn
ama nattō	sugar coated beans boiled in syrup
ama zake	sweet, warm sake
an	sweet bean paste
anko	beans boiled with sugar
bentō	lunch box with rice and different vegetables, meat, fish etc.
chāhan	fried rice
champon	noodle soup
daikon	Chinese radish
dango	round balls made from rice and flour
gohan	cooked rice/also a general term for 'meal'
gyōza	Chinese style dumplings, made from pork, cabbage, garlic ginger
gyūtan	beef tongue

ikizukuri	a method of presentation of fish/lobster in which fish is served alive
jun-maishu	Japanese rice wine made by grinding rice
kabayaki	grilled fish or eel dipped in shôyu based sauce
karē namban	buckwheat noodles with with chicken/pork curry
karē raisu	Japanese style curry and rice
karē udon	udon noodles with curry sauce
men	noodles
miso	fermented soy-bean paste, also made from rice or barley
miso rāmen	ramen with miso flavoured broth
miso shiru	soup made from miso paste with fish stock/ vegetables
mitsu mame	Japanese dessert made from boiled red peas, agar-agar and fruit
mochi	rice cake made from glutinous rice
omu raisu	omelette and rice
onigiri	rice ball
rāmen	yellow wheat noodles
sashimi	raw fish or meat
sushi	any food served on or rolled in vinegared rice

tempura	seafood, meat & vegetables deep fried in light batter
tempura soba	buckwheat noodles in broth with tempura pieces on top
tempura udon	wheat flour noodles in broth with tempura pieces on top
tendon	battered prawn on rice
wagashi	Japanese sweets
yaki mochi	toasted rice cake
yaki soba	fried noodles with vegetables & meat
yaki tori	grilled meat on skewers served with salt

Nature, Colours, Animals, Birds, Insects & Flowers

NATURE (SHIZEN)

English	Japanese
Air	kūki
Atmosphere	fun-iki
Beach	hamabe
Climate	kikō
Cloud	kumo
Earth	chikyū
Fire	hi
Fog	kiri
Forest	mori
Frost	shimo
Gale	kyōfū
Hail	arare
Heaven	tengoku
Hell	jigoku

Ice	kōri
Lake	mizūmi
Lightning	denkō
Milky Way	ginga
Moon	tsuki
Moonlight	gekkō
Mountain	yama
Ocean	kaiyō
Pollution	osen
Rain	ame
River	kawa
Sea	umi
Shade	kage
Shore	kaigan
Sky	sora
Star	hoshi
Storm	arashi
Stream	nagare
Sun	taiyō

Sunrise	hi-no-de
Sunset	hi-botsu
Sunshine	nikkō
Thunder	kaminari
Universe	uchyū
Water	mizu
Weather	tenki
World	sekai

PLANETS (WAKUSEI)

English	Japanese
Earth	chikyū
Jupiter	yupitaru
Mars	ka-sei
Mercury	sui-sei
Neptune	kaiō -sei
Pluto	meiō -sei
Saturn	do-sei
Uranus	tennō -sei
Venus	kin-sei

SEASONS, WEATHER, NATURE (KISETSU)

English	Japanese
Autumn	aki
Breezy	soyo kaze
Cloudy	kumoru
Cold	samui
Drizzle	koma ame
Earthquake	jishin
Hot	atsui
Humid	mushi atsui
Rain	ame
Rainy season	uki
Snow	yuki
Spring	haru
Summer	natsu
Sunny	hare
Typhoon	taifū
Volcanic eruption	funka

Volcano	kazan
Warm	atatakai
Weather	tenki
Weather forecast	tenki yohō
Wind	kaze
Winter	fuyu

The weather is good/bad today
Kyō wa ī/ warui tenki des

It is very hot/cold today!
Kyō wa totemo atsui/samui des

It is raining
Ame ga futte imas

Don't forget your umbrella!
Kasa o wasurenaide kudasai !

COLOURS (IRO)

English	Japanese
Bright	akarui
Blue	aoi
Black	kuroi
Brown	cha-iro
Gold	kin-iro
Green	midori
Olive	oribu
Pink	pinku
Purple	murasaki
Red	akai
White	shiroi

This is a blue shirt
Kore wa aoi shatsu des

ANIMALS (DŌBUTSU)

English	Japanese
Animal	dōbutsu
Bull	o-ushi
Buffalo	suigyū
Calf	ko-ushi
Cat	neko
Chameleon	kamereon
Camel	rakuda
Cow	ushi
Deer	shika
Dog	inu
Donkey	roba
Elephant	zō
Endangered	zetsumetsu ni sarasareta
Fox	kitsune
Goat (m)	yagi

Hare	no usagi
Heifer	me-ushi
Horse	uma
Hound	ryoken
Jackal	jakkaru
Lamb	ko-hitsuji
Leopard	hyō
Lion	ra-i-on
Mare	me-uma
Mongoose	manguzu
Monkey	saru
Mouse	nezumi
Mule	raba
Pig	buta
Pup	ko-inu
Python	nishiki hebi
Rabbit	usagi
Rhinoceros	sai
Sheep	hitsuji

Skunk	sukanku
Snake	hebi
Squirrel	risu
Swine	buta
Tiger	tora
Wolf	ōkami

This place is a zoo
Koko wa dōbutsuen des

This is an elephant
Kore wa zō des

WATER ANIMALS

English	Japanese
Crab	kani
Crocodile	wani
Fish	sakana
Leech	hiru
Tortoise	kame

This is a crab
Kore wa kani des

BIRDS (TORI)

English	Japanese
Bat	kōmori
Bird	tori
Cock	ondori
Crane	tsuru
Crow	karasu
Cuckoo(m)	kakkō
Dove	hato
Duck	ahiru
Hen	men-dori
Kite	tobi
Nightingale	nai-chingēru
Owl	fukurō
Parrot	ōmu
Partridge	yama uzura
Peacock	kujaku
Pigeon	hato
Sparrow	suzume
Swan	hakuchō
Vulture	hagewashi

INSECTS (MUSHI)

English	Japanese
Ant	ari
Bee	hachi
Bug	konchyū
Butterfly	chōchō
Firefly	hotaru
Fly	hae
Frog	kaeru
Germ	baikin
Insect	mushi
Lizard	yamori
Locust	batta
Mosquito	ka
Scorpion	sasori
Spider	kumo
Snail	katatsumuri
Wasp	jigabachi

FLOWERS (HANA)

English	Japanese
Acacia	akashia
Balsamo	barusa
Cherry blossom	sakura
Chrysanthemum	kiku
Conifer	sugi
Daisy	hinagiku
Jasmine	jasmin
Lilac	rira
Lily	yuri
Lotus	hasu
Magnolia	mokuren
Mushroom	kinoko
Myrtle	gibaika
Narcissus	suisen
Pine	matsu
Plum	ume
Rose	bara

ARTICLES & CLOTHING (IRYŌHIN)

English	Japanese
Air freshener	hōkōzai
Ash tray	haizara
Basket	kago
Bedsheet	beddo Shito
Bench	benchi
Bottle	bottoru
Box	bokkusu
Brush	fude
Bucket	baketsu
Candle	rōsoku
Canister	kan
Censer	kōro
Chair	isu
Chandelier	shanderia
Churner	nyūki
Cigarette-	tabako

Lighter	raitā
Comb	kushi
Cutlery	hamono
Deodorant	bōshūzai
Finger bowl	fingā bōru
Fork	fōku
Funnel	jōgo
Inkpot	inku ire
Jar	bin, Tsubo
Jug	mizu ire
Key	kagi
Knife	naifu
Ladle	hishaku
Lid	futa
Lock	jō
Mat	matto, tatami (Japanese style mat)
Match	macchi bako
Mirror	kagami

Needle	hari
Oven	ōbun
Pen	pen
Perfume	kōsui
Pestle	surikogi
Phial	kusuri bin
Pillow	makura
Pincers	yattoko
Plate	osara
Pot	hachi
Rope	nawa
Safe	kinko
Sieve	uragoshi-ki
Soap	sekken
Sack	ōbukuro
Shampoo	shanpū
Shower	shawā
Spittoon	tantsubo
Spoon	supūn

Stick	bō
Stool	koshigake
Stove	konro
String	himo
Table	tēburu
Table cloth	tēburu Kurosu
Thimble	yubi nuki
Tongs	yattoko
Tissue paper	tisshu pēpā
Tray	bon, torē
Tumbler	tanbura
Umbrella	kasa
Wire	harigane
Wick	shin

WRITING AND READING (DOKUSHO)

English	Japanese
Blotting paper	suitorigami
Book	hon
Card	kado
Clip	kurippu
Chalk	chōku
Cork	koruku
Crayon	kurēyon
Dividers	bunwari konpasu
Drawing pin	gabyō
Envelope	fūtō
Pile	kebo
Fountainpen	man-nen hitsu
Glue	nori
Gum	gomu
Ink	inku
Invitation-card	shōtaijō

Letter	tegami
Magazine	zasshi
Newspaper	shim-bun
Nib	pen saki
Paper	kami
Paper weight	bunchin
Pen	pen
Pencil	empitsu
Pen-knife	kaichū naifu
Quill pen	gapen
Receipt book	ryōshūsho-chō
Register	kiroku
Revenue stamp	shyūnyū inshi
Rubber	keshigomu
Seal	shīru, inkan*
Sealing wax	fūrō
Scissors	hasami
Stamps	kitte
Tag	fuda

Visiting card	meishi
Waste paper	kamikuzu

Where is the book shop?
Hon-ya wa doko des ka

I want to buy a book
Watashi wa hon o kaitai des

Can you give me a pen?
pen o kudasai

CLOTHING (FUKU)

English	Japanese
Apron	epuron
Bathing suit	suigi
Bathing trunks	suiei pantsu
Belt	beruto
Bikini	bikini
Blanket	mōfu
Blouse	burausu
Bra	burajā
Brocade	nishiki
Bodice	besuto
Border	heri
Button	botan
Boots	nagakutsu
Canvas	kyanbasu
Cap	bōshi
Cardigan	kādegan

Cashmere	kashimiya
Coat	uwagi
Chintz	chintsu
Cotton	wata
Cloak	manto
Cloth	nuno
Corduroy	kōruten
Corset	korusetto
Damask	damasuku-ori
Darning	tsukuroi
Dress	fuku, doresu
Flannel	furano
Gloves	tebukuro
Handkerchief	hankachi
Hat	bōshi
Jacket	uwagi, jaketto
Jersey	jāji
Knitted	an-da
Lace	himo

Leather	hikaku, kawa
Lining	urabari
Lingerie	ranjerī
Muffler	erimaki
Napkin	napukin
Nightgown	negurije
Pajamas	pajama
Pants	zubon
Panty	pantsu, shitagi
Parka	pāka
Petticoat	pechikōto
Polyester	poriesteru
Pocket	poketto
Quilt	kiruro
Raincoat	rein kōto
Satin	saten
Scarf	sukāfu
Serge	sāji
Shawl	shōru

Shirt	shatsu
Silk	kinu
Skirt	skāto
Sleeve	tamoto
Sportswear	supōtsu wea
Stitching	ami
Stocking	kutsushita
Suit	sūtsu
Thread	ito
Tie	nekutai
Towel	taoru
Trousers	zubon
Tunic	chunikku
Turban	tāban
Veil	beru
Velvet	berubetto
Wool	yōmō
Waistcoat	chokki
Yarn	amimono ito

MAKEUP, JEWELS AND ORNAMENTS (KESHŌHIN, HŌSEKI, SŌSHOKUHIN)

English	Japanese
Anklet	ashikubi no kazari
Armlet	ude-wa
Bangle	ude-wa
Bracelet	burēsuretto
Brooch	burōchi
Chain	kusari
Chignon	shi-niyon
Clip	kurippu
Earring	mimi-kazari
Hairpin	hea-pin
Locket	roketto
Mother of pearl	shinju-sō
Necklace	nekkuresu
Pendant	pendanto
Powder	kona
Ring	yubiwa

Scent	nioi
Tiara	tiara
Wristlet	udewa
Wrist watch	ude-dokei
Wreath	hanawa
Agate	menō
Coral	sango
Emerald	emerarudo
Gems	hōseki
Opal	opāru
Pearl	shinju
Pebble	koishi
Ruby	rubī
Sapphire	safaiya
Topaz	topāzu
Turquoise	toruo-ishi
Zircon	jirukon

MEDICAL VOCABULARY (BYŌKI)

English	Japanese
Accident	jiko
Acidity	sanmi
Acne	nikibi
Acupuncture	hari
AIDS	eizu
Ailments	byōki
Allergy	arerugi
Ambulance	kyūkyūsha
Anaesthetic	masui-zai
Antibiotics	kōsei-busshitsu
Anti-inflammatories	kōen shōyaku
Antihistamines	kō-hisutamin-zai
Appendicitis	chyūsui-en
Aromatherapy	aroma terapī
Aspirin	asupirin
Asthma	zensoku

Baldness	hage
Bandage	hōtai
Belching	geppu
Bile	tanjyū
Bleeding	shukketsu
Blindness	mōmoku
Blister	mizu-bukure
Blood group	ketsugata
Blood pressure	ketsuatsu
Breath	iki
Bronchitis	kikan-shien
Bruise	kizu
Burn	yakedo
Cardiac arrest	shinzō mahi
Cataract	hakunaishō
Casualty	higai-sha
Chemotherapy	kagaku ryōhō
Chickenpox	mizu bōsō
Chilblain	shimo-yake

Cholera	korera
Clinic	chinryō-jo
Colic	yoru naki
Concussion	nōshin-tō
Condom	kondōmu
Conjunctivitis	ketsumaku-en
Constipation	benpi
Consumption	hai-byō
Contraceptive	hinin-yaku
Cough	seki
Cramp	keiren
Cure	chiryō
Depression	utsu-byō
Dermatologist	hifu byōgaku-sha
Diabetes	tō -nyō -byō
Diagnosis	shinsatsu
Diarrhoea	geri
Disease	byōki
Dispensary	chōzai-shitsu

Dizziness	memai
Doctor	o-Isha
Dose	ippuku
Drugstore	yakkyoku
Dumbness	mugon
Dwarf	ko-bito
Dysentry	sekiri
Eczema	shisshin
ENT	jibi-in-kōka
Epidemic	densen-byō
Epilepsy	tenkan
Faint	shisshin
Fever	netsu
Filling	tsume mono
First aid	ōkyū
Fistula	rō
Flu	infuruenza
Food poisoning	shokudoku
Fungal	kin

Giddiness	memai
Gland	sen
Gonorrhoea	rinbyō
Griping	kirikiri-suru
Have cold	kaze o hiku
Headache	zutsū
Hernia	herunia
Hiccup	shakkuri
High blood pressure	kō-ketsuatsu
Homeopathy	homeopashī
Hospital	byōin
Hunger	kiga
Indigestion	ijaku
Infection	densen
Inflammation	enshō
Insomnia	fumin-shō
Itch	kayui
Jaundice	ōdan
Kidney stone	jinzō kesseki

Leprosy	hansen-byō
Leukaemia	hakketsu-byō
Madness	kyō-ki
Measles	hashika
Medicine	kusuri
Menstruation	gekkei
Migraine	henzutsū
Mumps	jikasen-en
Naturopathy	shizen ryōhō
Nausea	haki-ke
Operation	shujutsu
Pain	itami
Paralysis	mahi
Penicillin	penishirin
Pharmacy	seiyaku
Phlegm	tan
Piles	ji
Plaster	purastā
Pneumonia	haien

Pregnant	nimpu
Prescription	shohō
Pulse	myaku
Pus	umi
Reflexology	rifurekusoroji
Reiki	reiki
Rheumatism	ryūmachi
Ringworm	hakusen
Roundworm	kaichyū
Saliva	da-eki
Sanitary napkin	seiri-yō napukin
Short sighted 1ess	kinshi-gan
Sick	byōki
Side effect	fuku-sayō
Sinusitis	fukubi-kōen
Sleeping pill	suiminyaku
Sneeze	kushami
Sore throat	inkōen
Sprain	nenza
Stomachache	fukutsū

Stool	daiben
Sunburn	hiyake
Sunstroke	nisshabyō
Surgery	shujutsu
Sweat	ase
Swelling	hare
Syringe	chyūsha-ki
Tablet	jō-zai
Tetanus	hashō-fū
Thermometer	ondokei
Treatment	chiryō
Tumour	shuyō
Typhus	hasshin chifusu
Urine	nyō
Vaccination	wakuchin
Vomiting	haku
Ward	byōtō
Weak	yowai
Wheelchair	kuruma Isu
Wound	kega
X-ray	ekkusu-re

SPORTS (SUPŌTSU)

English	Japanese
Aikido	aikidō (Japanese martial art form)
Archery	kyūdō
Athletics	rikujō kyōgi
Badminton	badominton
Ball	bōru
Baseball	yakyū
Basketball	basuketto Bōru
Bat	batto
Bullfight	tōgyū
Champion	yūshō-sha
Championship	senshu-ken
Coach	kōchi
Corner	kōnā
Cricket	kuriketto
Defeat	make
Football	sakkā
Game	shiai/gēmu

Goal	gōru
Goalkeeper	gōru kīpā
Group	gurū-pu
Hockey	hokkē
Judo	jyūdō
Karate	karate
Kendo	kendō
Martial art	budō
Match	shiai
Mountain biking	maunten baiku
Offside	ofusaido
Penalty	penarute
Player	senshu
Playground	asobi-ba
Racket	raketto
Sportsman	supōtsu-man
Sumo	sumō
Swimming	suiei
Table tennis	takkyū
Team	chīmu
Tennis	tesnisu

Tennis court	tenisu kōto
Victory	kachi
Volleyball	barebōru
Winner	shōri-sha
Wrestling	resuringu, sumō (Japanese style wrestling)

What sport do you play?
Donna supōtsu o shimas ka

What sport do you follow?
Dono supōtsu no fan des ka

Do you like sumo/football/cricket/baseball?
Sumō/kuriketto/yakyūga ski des ka

I like watching sports.
Watshi wa supōtsu o miru no ga ski des

Who is your favorite sportsperson/team?
Dono senshu ga ichiban ski des ka

What is the score?
Skoa wa dō des ka

ART & ENTERTAINMENT (BIJUTSU)

English	Japanese
Actor	haiyū
Actress	joyū
Antique (Japanese)	kottō-hin
Architecture	kenchiku
Art	bijutsu
Artist	gaka
Audience	kankyaku
Calligraphy	shodō
Ceramics	tōgei
Critic (art)	hyōronka
Curator	kyurētā
Dance	odori
Dancer	dansā
Design	dezain
Drama	dorama
Essay	sakubun
Essayist	zuihitsu-ka
Exhibit	tenran

Film	eiga
Flower arranging	ikebana
Folk art	mingei
Folk dance	minzoku buyō
Folk music	minzoku ongaku
Folk tale	mukashi Banashi
Garden design	zōen
Installation	instarēshon
Ink painting	suiboku-ga
Japanese dolls	ningyō
Lacquerware	shikki
Literature	bungaku
Narrative epics	monogatari
Music	ongaku
Musician	ongaku-ka
Novel	shōsetsu
Novelist	shōsetsu-ka
Opening	ōpuningu
Opera	opera
Opera house	opera gekiba

Painter	gaka
Painting (work of art)	e
Painting (technique)	kai-ga
Period	jidai
Poet	shijin
Print	insatsu
Sculptor	chōkoku-ka
Sculpture	chōkoku
Song	uta
Statue	zō
Story	hanashi
Studio	sutajio
Style	sutairu
Tattoo art	ire-zumi
Tea ceremony	sadō
Technique	gi-jutsu
Textiles	kiji
Theater	en-geki
Woodblock prints	hanga
Writer	sakka

AROUND TOWN
(Some General Vocabulary)

English	Japanese
Airport	kūkō
Amusement park	yūen-chi
Antique shop	ko-bijutsu-ten
Asylum	seishin byōin
Bakery	pan-ya
Bar	sakaba
Bazaar	ichiba
Beauty parlor	biyō-in
Bicycle	jitensha
Boarding house	geshuku-ya
Bookshop	hon-ya
Border	sakai
Bridge	hashi
Building	biru
Bus	basu
Bus-shelter	teiryū-jo

Café	kissaten
Carpentry	daimoku
Cart	ni-basha
Cellular phone	keitai denwa
Chemist	kusuri-ya
Church	kyōkai
Cigarette	tabako
Cinema-hall	ei-ga-kan
Circus	sākasu
Club	kurabu
Concert hall	ongaku-dō
Court (law)	saibansho
Crossing (road)	kōsa-ten
Crowd	hito-gomi
Ditch (road)	mizo
Embassy	taishi-kan
Electricity	denki
Excursion	ensoku
Exhibition	tenran-kai

Factory	kōjyō
Farm	nōjō
Fence	saku
Festival	matsuri
Field (meadow)	hara
Flea market	nomi no ichi
Flower	hana
Fort	(o) shiro
Fountain	funsui
Fund	zandaka
Furniture shop	kagu-ya
Gallery (art)	bijutsu-kan
Garden	niwa
Give	ageru
Grave	(o) haka
Gutter	haisui-ro
Ground	jimen
Harbour	minato
Highrise building	kōsō biru

Highway	kōsoku dōro
Hill	oka
Hospital	byōin
Hotel	hoteru
House	ie, uchi
Hut	koya
ID	mibun shōmeisho
Industry	kōgyō
Inn	ryokan
Joke	jyōdan
Kindergarten	yōchi-en
Lane (town)	roji
Library	toshokan
Mosque	mosuku
Motorcycle	ōtobai
Mountain	yama
Mountaineering	tozan
Mountain range	san-myaku
Museum	hakubutsu-kan

Name	namae
Orphanage	koji-in
Park	kōen
Pawnshop	shichi-ya
Place	basho/tokoro
Plants	shokubutsu
Police	keisatsu
Police station	keisatsu-sho
Police box	kōban
Poster	bira
Post office	yūbin-kyoku
Prefecture	ken
Problem	mondai
Public telephone	kōshyūdenwa
Receive	morau/ukeru
Restaurant	restoran
Rickshaw	rikisha
River	kawa
Road	michi

Savings	chokin
School	gakkō
Scooter	sukūtā
Sea	umi
Shop	mise
Stadium	sutajia
Station	eki
Street (big)	dōro
Street (small)	michi
Swimming pool	suiei pūru
Tailor	yōsai-shi
Take	toru
Taxi	takushī
Telegraph	denpō
Telephone	denwa
Temple	otera
Three-wheeler	sanrin-sha
Ticket	chiketto, kippu
Tomb	haka, reibyō

Tourism	kankō
Tourist	kankō-kyaku
Tower	tawā, tō
Town	machi
Toy	omocha
Traffic	kōtsū
Traffic jam	kōtsū jyūtai
Traffic lights	shingō
Traffic sign	kōtsū hyōshiki
Train	densha
Tram	toramu
Tree	ki
Truck	torakku
University	daigaku
Valley	tani
Village	mura
Wall	kabe
Ward	ku
Zoo	dōbutsu-en

DIRECTIONS (HŌKŌ)

English	Japanese
Behind	ushiro
Besides	tonari
Down	shita
East	higashi
Far away	tōi
Here	koko
In front of	mae ni
Left	hidari
Middle	naka, chyū
Near	chikaku ni
Next to	soba ni
North	kita
North-east	hokutō
North-west	hokusei
Right	migi
South	minami

South-east	nantō
South-west	nansei
Straight ahead	massugu
There	asoko
Turn	magaru
Turn left	hidari ni magaru
Turn right	migi ni magaru
Up	ue
West	nishi

Where is the......
.....wa doko des ka

How do I get there?
Dō ikeba ī des ka

How far is it?
Dono kurai no kyori des ka

What is the address?
Jyūsho wa nan des ka

ON THE PLANE/AT THE AIRPORT

English	Japanese
Aircraft	hiksōki
Airport	kūkō
Airsickness	hikōki yoi
Arrival	tōchaku
Cancel	kyanseru
Charter flight	chāta bin
Check in	chekku in
Connecting flight	setsuzoku-bin
Crew	jōmuin
Custom clearance	zeikan kuriaransu
Custom duty	kanzei
Custom inspection	zeikan kensa
Delay	chikoku
Daparture	shuppatsu
Departure lounge	machiai-shitsu, kyūkei-shitsu

Departure time	shuppatsu jikan
Destination	yukusaki
Domestic flight	kokunai-bin
Duty-free	kanzei nashi
Duty-free shop	menzei-ten
Economy class	ekonomi kurasu
Emergency exit	hijyō-guchi
Excess baggage	chyōka te-nimotsu
Fare	ryōkin
First class	ittō
Flight	furaito, -bin
Flight attendant	jōmuin
Fog	kiri
Hand luggage	te nimotsu
Helicopter	herikoputā
Information	jyōhō
Land	chakuriku
Landing	chakuriku suru
Life-jacket	kyūmei dōi

Luggage	nimotsu
Non-stop flight	chokkō-bin
Passenger	jyōkyaku
Passport	pasupōto
Pilot	sōjyū-shi
Plane	hikōki
Return ticket	ōfuku kippu
Round trip	ōfuku ryokō
Route	keiro
Seatbelt	shīto beruto
Shuttle service	shattaru sābisu
Take off	ririku
Ticket	chiketto, ken
Visa	biza
Wing	tsubasa

May I see your passport please?
Pasupōto o mite mo ī des ka

That is not mine
Sore wa watashino dewa arimasen

That is mine
Sore wa watashino des

I have something to declare
Shinsei suru mono ga arimas

I have nothing to declare
Nani mo shinsei suru mono ga arimasen

Are you Indian?
Anatawa indo jin des ka

I am here on business/holiday
Watashiwa bijinesu/yasumi no tame koko ni kimashta

Where do you want to go?
Doko e ikitai des ka

COUNTRIES (KUNI)

English	Japanese
America	amerika
American	amerika jin
Argentina	aruzenchin
Asia	ajia
Asian	ajia jin
Australia	ōsutoraria
Australian	ōsutoraria jin
Brazil	burajiru
Chile	chiri
China	chūgoku
Chinese	chūgokujin
Christian	kurischan
Country	kuni
Empire	teikoku
England	igirisu
Europe	yōroppa
European	yōroppa-jin
Flag	hata

France	furansu
French	furansu jin
Germany	doitsu
German	doitsu jin
Hindu	hinzū
India	indo
Indian	indo jin
Japan	nihon
Japanese	nihon jin
Kingdom	ōkoku
Motherland	bokoku
Muslim	isuramu-kyōto
Nation	kokka
Patriotism	aikokushin
Portugal	porutogaru
Portuguese	po-ru-to-garu jin
Province	shyū
Spain	supein
Spanishs	supein jin
State	kokka

POLITICS, SOCIETY, RELIGION (SEIJI, SHAKAI, SHYV̄KYŌ)

English	Japanese
Candidate	kōho-sha
Communist	kyō-san
Conservative	ho-shu
Democratic	min-shu
Election	senkyo
Liberal	ji-yū
Liberal democrat	ji-min
Parliament	kokkai, gikai
Politics	seiji
Politician	seiji-ka
Social democratic	shakai min-shu
Society	sha-kai

Political parties

DPJ (democratic party of Japan)	min-shu-tō
JCP(Japanese communist party)	kyō-san-tō
LDP(Liberal democratic party)	ji-min-tō
SDP(Social democratic party)	shamin-tō

SOCIETY (SHAKAI)

English	Japanese
Abortion	hinin
Animal rights	dōbutsu no kenri
Conservation	shizen hogo
Corruption	oshoku
Crime	hanzai
Deforestation	shinrin bassai
Discrimination	sabetsu
Drought	kangai
Drugs	mayaku
Economy	keizai
Education	kyōiku
Environment	kankyō
Euthanasia	anrakushi
Foreigner	gaikokujin
Globalisation	guro¯baru-ka/koksai-ka
Human rights	jinken

Hunting	shuryō
Immigration	imin
Inequality	fubyōdō
Pollution	kōgai
Poverty	hinkon
Privatisation	minei-ka
Racism	jinshu sabetsu
Recycling	risaikuru
Sexism	sei sabetsu
Social welfare	shakai fukushi
Suicide	jisatsu
Terrorism	tero
Unemployment	shitsugyō-ka
War	sensō

RELIGION (SHYŪKYŌ)

English	Japanese
Agnostic	fukachiron-ja
Astrology	hoshi uranai
Atheist	mushinron-ja
Attend mass	misa ni sanka
Buddhism	bukkyō
Buddhist	bukkyō-to
Catholic	katorikku kyōto
Church	kyōkai
Christian	kirisuto kyōto
Fate	unmei
God	kami
Hindu	hinzu kyōto
Jewish	yudaya kyōto
Meditate	meisō
Mosque	mosusku
Muslim	isuramu kyōto

Pray	o-inori
Shinto	shintō
Temple	o-tera/ji-in
Worship	reihai

HOBBIES (SHUMI)

English	Japanese
Billiards	biriyādo
Hobby	shumi
Cooking	ryōri
Dancing	odori
Drawing	skecchi
Films	eiga
Gardening	zōen
Hiking	haikingu
Music	ongaku
Painting	kaiga
Photography	shashin
Reading	dokusho
Shopping	kaimono
Socialize	o-shaberi
Sports	supōtsu
To like	ski

Travelling	ryokō
TV	terebi

What is your hobby?
Anatano shumi wa nan des ka

Do you like music?
Anatawa ongaku ga ski des ka

Do you like traveling?
Anatawa ryokō ga ski des ka

Do you like movies?
Anatawa eiga ga ski des ka

RELATIONSHIP (KANKEI)

English	Japanese
Adopted	yōshi
Aunt	o-ba
Boyfriend	koibito
Bride	hana-yome
Bridegroom	hana-muko
Child	kodomo
Cousin	itoko
Daughter	musume
Elder brother	onisan
Elder sister	onēsan
Family	kazoku
Father	otōsan/chichi
Fiancé	kon-yaku-sha
Friend	tomodachi
Girlfriend	koibito
Grandchildren	ago

Granddaughter	mago musume
Grand parents	so-fu/so-bo
Grandson	mago musuko
Guest	o-kyaku sama
Husband	shujin
Marriage	kekkon
Marriage ceremony	kokkeon-shiki
Mother	okāsan/haha
Nieghbour	rinjin
Nephew	oi
Niece	mei
Parents	ryōshin
Relative	shin-seki
Sister	shimai
Son	musuko
Spouse	haigū-sha
Twin	futa-go
Uncle	oji-san
Wedding	kekkon

Widow	mi-bō-jin
Wife	oksan
Younger brother	otōto
Younger sister	imōto

This is my father
Kochira wa watashino chichi des

She is my mother
Kochira wa watashino haha des

She is my wife
Kochira wa watashino oksan des

I have two children
Kodomo ga futari imas

He is my uncle
Kochira wa watashino ojisan des

Do you have a brother/sister?
Go kyōdai/shimai ga imas ka

How many brothers do you have?
Kyōdai wa nan-nin imas ka

I have two brothers.
Kyōdai ga futari imas

She is my younger sister
Kochira wa watashino imōto des

Are you married?
Kekkon shite imas ka

I am living-in with someone.
Watashi wa dōsei shite imas

I am single/divorced
Watashi wa dokshin desu/rikon shimashta

OCCUPATION/STUDIES (SHOKUGYŌ)

English	Japanese
Businessman	bijines-man
Company	kaisha
Chef	shefu
Doctor	o-isha
Employee	kaisha-in
Farmer	nōmin
Fisherman	ryōshi
Homemaker	shufu
Journalist	jānaristo
Lawyer	bengoshi
Office	jimusho/ ofisu
Public servant	kōmuin
Retired	taishoku-sha
Self employed	jieigyō-sha
Student	gakusei
Study	benkyō

Teacher	sensei/kyōshi
Unemployed	shitsugyō-sha

What are you studying?
Nani o benkyōshite imas ka

I am studying science/geography/maths/sociology
Watashi wa kagaku/chiri-gaku/sū-gaku/shakai-gaku

I am a businessman/student/teacher
Watashi wa bijinesuman/gakusei/sensei des

JAPANESE CULTURE, ART, TRADITION

I guess most of us are familiar with words like kimono, sumo, and karaoke etc. even without knowing Japanese language. Below is a list of words that are originally Japanese but are known worlwide, and sometimes used in other languages as well. A detailed explanation would not be possible here due to space restriction.

Bonsai	the art of cultivating trees in a tray (bon)
Bunraku	puppet thatre of Japan
Go	A popular board game of japan
Haiku	shortest form of poetry (17 syllable)
Ikebana	The art of flower arrangement
Kabuki	Japanese thatre, distant similarity with 'Kathakali'
Karaoke	literally 'empty orchestra'. A favorite pastime of the Japanese.
Manga	this word is a part of the English lexicon now. Means ' cartoons'
Nō	Zen influenced dance-drama
Origami	the art of paper folding to make various objects
Pachinko	probably the favorite pastime of Japanese, another form of gambling.

Shōgi	Japanese form of chess
ukiyo-e	a type of wood block print
waka	A 31 syllable poem in Japanese
washi	Japanese paper
yamato-e	Japanese painting
zen	Japanised form of buddhism with an overt emphasis on simplicity.

PROVERBS (KOTOWAZA)

It is said that a culture's proverbs can be seen as a reflection on how people think. Read the proverbs below and see if you can correlate the Japanese way of thinking with your own.

1. 出るくぎはうたれる *Deru kugi wa utareru.*

Meaning: The nonconformist will be pounded down. / Don't make waves.

2 サルも木から落ちる *Saru mo ki kara ochiru.*

Meaning: Everyone makes mistakes. / Nobody's perfect.

3. 猫に小判 *neko ni koban*

Meaning: casting pearls before swine.

4. 七転び八起き *nanakorobi yaoki*

Meaning: Life is full of ups and downs.

5. 三日坊主 *mikka bōzu*

Meaning:Giving up at the first sign of difficulty.

6. 晴耕雨読 *seiko udoku*

Meaning:Farm when it's sunny, read when it rains.

7. 十人十色 *jūnin toiro*

Meaning: To each his/her own. / Different strokes for different folks.

8. 悪因悪果 *akuin akka*

Meaning: Sow evil and reap evil.

9. 大同小異 *daidō shōi*

Meaning: Similarities outweigh the differences.

10. 一石二鳥 *isseki nichō*

Meaning: Killing two birds with one stone.

11. 風は万病の元 *kaze wa manbyō no moto*

Meaning: A cold leads to all kinds of diseases

12. 学問に王道なし *gakumon ni ōdō nashi*

Meaning: There is no royal road to learning

13. 金は天下の回りもの *kane wa tenka no mawari mono*

Meaning: Money comes and goes

14. 蛙の子は蛙 *kaeru no ko wa kaeru*

Meaning: Like father, like son

15. 飼い犬に手を噛まれる *kai-inu ni te o kamareru*

Meaning: Bite the hand that feeds

16. 短気は損気 *tanki-wa son-ki*

A short temper helps nothing

17. 便りのないのはよい便り *tayori no nai no-wa yoi tayori*

No news is good news

18. 膝とも談合 *Hiza tomo dangō.*

Two heads are better than one.

19. 頂くものは夏でも小袖 *Itadaku mono wa natsu de mo kosode.*

Don't look a gift horse in the mouth.

20. 郷に入っては郷に従え *Gō ni itte wa gō ni shitagae.*

When in Rome, do as the Romans do.

21. 船頭多くて船山に登る *Sendō ōku shite fune yama ni noboru.*

Too many cooks spoil the broth.

22. 矯めるなら若木のうち *Tameru nara wakagi no uchi.*

"While young, the tree can be easily bent."

23. 相手のない喧嘩はできぬ *Aite no nai kenka wa dekinu.*

"One can't quarrel without an opponent."

24. 千里の行も一歩より始まる（老子） *Senri no kō mo ippo yori hajimaru*

"A thousand ri (roughly one-third of a mile) journey begins with a single step."

25. 二足の草鞋を履く *Nisoku no waraji o haku.*

"To wear two pairs of straw sandals at once" (wearing "two hats" at the same time)

26. 生き恥かくより 死ぬがまし *Ikihaji kaku yori, shinu ga mashi.*

"Better to die than to live in shame."

27. 教えるは学ぶの半ばなり *Oshieru wa manabu no nakaba nari.*

"Teaching is half learning."

28. 百語より一笑 *hyakugo yori isshyō*

" A smile is worth a thousand words"

29. 聞き上手は話し上手 *kiki jyōzu wa hanashi jyōzu.*

" He who listens well, speaks well"

30. 笑顔は心の光です *egao wa kokoro no hikari des.*

" A smile radiates from the heart"

C. PRACTICAL JAPANESE

AT THE POST OFFICE

- Stamp - *kitte*
- Letter - *tegami*
- Post card - *hagaki*
- Envelope - *fūtō*
- Box - *hako*
- Surface mail (by Sea) - *funa bin*
- Air mail - *kō kū bin*
- Package - *kozutsumi*

USEFUL PHRASES

- *kitte kudasai*
  Please give me a stamp

- *~ made onegaishimas*
  Please send to ______ (*amerika*, *kanada*, *igirisu...*)

- *okuri tai*
  I want to send (something)

- *kore o okuri tain des ga...*
  I would like to send this. (more polite)

- *kore wa daijōbu des ka?*
  Is this ok?

- *itsu todokimas ka?*
  When will it arrive?

- *o ikura des ka*
  How much is it? (The 'o' at the beginning makes it polite)

ON THE TELEPHONE

Hello, this is nisha speaking.
Moshi moshi, kochira wa nisha des ga

Whose call is it?
Dare no denwa des ka

Can I speak to?
... san o onegai shimas

Call from tokyo.
Tōkyō kara no denwa des

Who do you want to speak to?
Donata ni kawarimas ka

You have the wrong number.
Sumimasen ga machigae denwa des

Is Mr tanaka there?
Tanaka san ga irasshaimas (imas) ka

Could you put me through to Mr suzuki?
Suzuki san ni kawatte itadekemas (moraemas) ka

Can I take a message for him?
Dengon o uketorimas

Can I leave a message for him?
Dengon o onegai dekimas ka

Could you give me the number of . . .?
... no denwa bangō o oshiete itadakemas ka

Would you repeat the number, please?
Bangō wa mō ichi sdo onegai shimas

It's engaged/busy
o-hanashi chyū des

What is the code for India?
Indo no kokubangō wa namban des ka

Can I dial direct to Mumbai?
Mumbai e chokusetsu denwa dekimas ka

You can dial the number direct.
Chokusetsu kakeru koto ga dekimas

I want to make an international call.
Koksai denwa o shitai no des ga

I have been cut off.
Denwa ga kiremashta

There is no reply from . . .
... kara ōtō ga arimasen

Please hold the line.
Chotto matte kudasai

I cannot get through.
Setuzoku dekimasen

AT THE HOTEL

AT THE RECEPTION
(uketsuke de)

-Do you have any accomodation available?
Heya no yoyaku dekimas ka

-I would like to book a room please
heya no yoyaku o onegai shimas

-Yes, please check in here.
Kochira no hō chekku auto shite kudasai

I have a prior reservation
Yoyaku ga arimas

-Single room or double?
Shinguru rūmu ni shimas ka, mata wa daburu rūmu ni shimas ka

-A.c or non a.c
eakon-tsuki ni shimas ka mata wa eakon nashi ni shimas ka

-I would prefer the top/ground/first floor,please.
Toppu/ikkai/nikai no heya o onegai shimas

-Room service, please.
Rūmu sābisu onegai shimas

-What is the check out time?
Chekku auto taimu wa nan-ji des ka

-For 5 nights/ weeks
go-haku/ go shyūkan

-How much for one night/person/week?
Ippaku/hitori/isshyūkan wa ikura des ka

-Do I have to pay in advance?
Mae-barai des ka

-When is breakfast served?
Chôshoku no jikan wa itsu des ka

-Please wake me at...
... ni okoshite kudasai

-Do you change money here?
Koko de ryōgae dekimas ka

-Can you call a taxi?
Takushī o yonde itadakemas ka

-Can I use the kitchen/telephone/laundry?
Daidokor/denwa/setntaku-ki o tsukatte mo ī des ka

AT MARKET/PUBLIC PLACES

-Have you any bananas?
Banana ga arimasu ka

-How much does this cost?
Kore wa ikura des ka

-It costs 5000 yen
kore wa go sen-en des

-That is costly!
Sore wa takai des!

-We can offer you a special rate/discount rate
waribiki/tokka dekimas

- I am lost
watashi wa mayotte imas

-Turn right/left
migi/hidari ni magatte kudasai

-Is this seat taken?
Kono seki ga aite imas ka

ANNOUNCEMENTS

-Everybody, Please take your seats.
Minasan! Chakuseki shite kudasai

-Open to the public on Mondays
getsuyōbi ni eigyō itashimas

-The train will arrive soon
Densha ga mamonaku hassha/tōchaku shimas

-The shops open at 9
mise wa ku-ji kara eigyō shimas

-Discount of 10%
juppasento no waribiki

SIGNS
AIRPORT

移民 Imin	immigration
検疫 Keneki	quarantine
出入国管理 Shutsunyūkoku kanri	passport control
税関 Zeikan	customs
免税 menzei	duty free

CITY (MACHI)

一時停止	ichiji teishi	stop here!
一方通行	ippō tsūkō	one way
入口	iriguchi	entrance
工事中	kōjichyū	men at work/under construction
立入禁止	tachi iri kinshi	no entry/no trespassing
駐車	chyūsha	parking
駐車禁止	chyūsha kinshi	no parking
出口	deguchi	exit
止まれ	tomare	stop!
料金所	ryōkinjo	toll
営業中	eigyōchyū	open (shops, restaurants)
男	otoko	men
女	onna	women
開館	kaikan	open (theatres,museums)

危険	kiken	danger
喫煙	kitsuen	smoking
禁煙	kin-en	no smoking
さわるな	sawaru na!	Do not touch
準備中	jumbi chyū	In preparation (restaurants)
トイレ	toire	toilets
入場無料	nyūjyō muryō	entry free
非常口	hijyō guchi	emergency exit
閉館	heikan	closed (theatres,museums etc.)
閉店	heiten	closed (shops, restaurants etc.)
満室	manshitsu	full/no vacancy
遊泳禁止	yūei kinshi	No swimming

SMALL TALK (OSHABERI)

Good morning, sir/madam!
Ohayō gozaimas

How are you?
O genki des ka

Very well.
Hai, genki des

What is your name?
o-namae wa nan des ka

My name is...
Watashimo namae wa....

Where do you come from?
Dochira kara koraremashita ka

I am from India
Indo kara mairimashta/indo kara kimashta

Do you live here?
Koko ni sunde imas ka

Where are you going?
Doko e ikimas ka

What are you doing?
Nani o shite imas ka

What business are you in?
Donna bijinesu o shite imas ka

Do you speak English?
Eigo dekimas ka/ eigo de hanasemas ka

I don't understand Japanese
Watashiwa nihongo ga wakarimasen

Could you please speak more slowly?
Mō chotto yukkuri hanashte moraemas ka

I can't speak japanese.
Watashi wa nihongo de hanasemasen

I speak a little japanese.
Watashi-wa nihongo ga sukoshi hanasemas

Are you married?
Go-kekkon shite imas ka

Yes, I am married. No. I am not married
Hai, kekkon shite imas/ īe, kekkon shite imasen

When is your birthday?
o-tanjōbi wa itsu des ka

What is your age?
o-ikutsu des ka/ nan sai des ka

I am 28 years old.
Watashiwa nijyū hassai des

What do you do?
Ima nani o shite imas ka

I am a student
Watashiwa gaksei des

Have you come here for the first time?
Koko ni hajimete kimashta ka

How long do you plan to stay?
Itsu made iru yotei deska/ itsumade koko ni iru tsumori-des ka

Another week.
Ato isshyū -kan

It is very nice here.
Koko wa subarashī des/ totemo ī des

It was nice meeting you.
Aete yokatta des/ o-ai dekite ureshī des

Keep in touch.
Renraku o tori torimashō

With great pleasure..
ō-yorokobi de..

Ok (all right)
Hai,ī des/ hai, daijō bu des

I am ok, thanks for asking.
Daijyō bu des. Kīte arigatō

Were you waiting for me?
Watashi o matte imashta ka

I don't like that
Watashiwa sore ga ski dewa arimasen

No thanks
Īe, kekkō des

I have no fixed plans
Toku ni yotei ga arimasen

Wait a moment!
Chotto matte!

It does not matter
Sorewa taishita koto dewa arimasen/kamaimasen

Tomorrow is my last day here.
Ashitawa koko ni iru saigo no hi des

I am here with my family
Koko ni kazoku to isshyo ni imasu

I would like you to meet...
.... O shōkai shimas

This is my child/colleague.
Kochira wa watashino kodomo/dōryō des

This is my friend
Kochira wa watashino tomodachi des

This is my wife/husband
Kochira wa watshino shujin/tsuma des

SOCIALISING (OSHABERI)

Are you free tomorrow?
Ashta hima des ka/ ashta jikan arimas ka

What are you doing today/this evening?
Kyō/komban wa nani o shimas ka

What are you doing now?
Ima nani o shite imas ka

Would you like to go for a meal/drink?
Shokuji/ nomi ni ikimasen ka

Can you come to dinner?
Yûshoku ni kite moraemas ka

I will pick you up.
Watashiwa mukae ni kimas

Are you ready?
Yōi dekimashta ka

Yes, I am ready
Hai, dekimashta

Let me treat you to a drink.
Watashiwa ogorimas

Will you join me for a drink?
Isshyō ni nomimasen ka

Would you like to go for a walk?
Sanpo shi ni ikimas ka

May I join you?
Watashi ga kuwawatte mo ī des ka

Ok!
Hai, ī des yo!

I feel like going out somewhere.
Doko ka e ikitai des/ikō to omotte imas

Let us go for a movie
Eiga o mi ni ikimashō

LOCAL TALK

English	Japanese
Hey!	oi
Great!	sugoi
Sure	mochiron
Maybe	tabun
So-so	mā-mā
No way!	dame
Ok	ī des yo
No problem	daijyō bu des
Good luck	gambatte
Joking	jyō dan des
really?	hontō des ka
What!	nani

AT THE BANK

What time does the bank open?
Ginkō wa nan-ji ni hirakimas ka

I would like to withdraw money.
Genkin/okane o hikidashtai des

I would like to cash a cheque
Kogitte no genkinka o onegai shimas

I would like to change a traveller's cheque
Toraberāzu chekku no genkinka o onegai shimas

What is the exchange rate?
Kawase rēto wa okura des ka

Where is the ATM?
ATM wa doko des ka

Can I have smaller notes?
Okane o kuzushte moraemas ka

Has my money arrived?
Okane wa todoite imas ka

DOING BUSINESS

I am attending a conference/meeting
Kaigi/mītingu ni shusseki shimas

Here is my business card
Watashino meishi des

What is your FAX number/mobile number/
E-mail address?
Anatano fakkusu bangō/keitai bangō/
ī mēru wa nan des ka

I have an appointment with Mr....
... san to apo ga arimas

EATING OUT

Can you recommend a bar/restaurant?
Doko ka ī restoran/bā o shitte imas ka

I would like to reserve a table for one person/two people.
Hitori/futari no yoyaku o onegai shimas

I would like to have the menu in English please.
Eigo no menyū o onegai shimas

How much is the waiting time?
Dono kurai machimas ka

I will have that
Kore ni shimas

What is in that dish?
Ano ryōri ni wa nani ga haitte imas ka

I am a vegetarian
Watashi wa saishokushugi-sha des

Is it self service?
Serufusābisu des ka

Bill please
Kanjō onegai shimas

I suggest the...
... wa watashino susume des

Do you have...?
.... Ga arimas ka

Please bring a spoon/knife/glass/cloth
Supūn/naifu/gurasu/fukin o kudasai

It was delicious!
Oishikatta des yo

This is spicy/cold/hot
Kore wa karai/tsumetai/atsui des!

I am full
Onaka ga ippai des

I will buy you a drink
Watashi wa nomimono o ogorimas

I would like a cup of tea/coffee/lemonade
Watashi wa o-cha/kōhī/remonēdo o nomitai des

Cheers!
Kampai!

I am drunk
Yopparatte imas

I feel ill
Kibun ga warui des

EMERGENCY (DOCTOR/POLICE/HOSPITAL)

HELP!
Tasukete!

Watch out!
Abunai!

It is an emergency
Kinkyū des

There has been an accident
Jiko ga arimashta

Call the police/doctor/ambulance
Keisatsu/o-isha/kyūkyū-sha o yonde kudasai

Can you help me?
Tasukete kudasai

I am lost
Watashi wa mayotte imas

Is it safe?
Anzen des ka

Where is the police station?
Keisatsu-sho wa doko des ka

I have been robbed
Watashi wa gōtō ni aimashta

I am sorry
Gomen nasai

Where is the nearest chemist/hospital/clinic?
Ichiban chikaku no yakkyoku/byōin/ kurinikku wa doko des ka

I have insurance
Hoken ni kakete arimas

What is the problem?
Nani ga mondai des ka/d ō shimashta ka

Do you drink/smoke?
Anatawa sake o nomimas ka/ tabako o suimas ka

Are you allergic to anything?
Arerugī ga arimas ka

I am sick
Watashi wa byōki des

I feel depressed/weak
Watashi wa yū-utsu des/chikara ga arimasen

I can't sleep
Watashi wa nemuremasen

I am pregnant
Watashi wa ninshin shite imas

COMPLAINTS

The door does not close properly
Doa wa chan to shimemasen

Please have it repaired
Kore o naoshite itadakemas ka

The air conditioner/fan does not work
Eakon/sempūki ga kowarete imas

The toilet is not clean
Toire wa kirei dewa arimasen

There is a cockroach in the bathroom
Furoba/toire ni gokiburi ga arimas

The room is too dark/bright
Kono heya wa kurasugimas/akarusugimas

The room is too cold/small
Kono heya wa samusugimas/chīsasugimas

Can I get another blanket
Mōfu o mō hitotsu onegai dekimās ka

WELL WISHING

English	Japanese
Bon voyage!	yoi tabi o
Congratulations!	omedetō gozaimas
Good luck!	gambatte
Happy birthday!	tanjōbi omedetō gozaimas
Happy new year!	akemashte omedetō
Hooray!	ban-zai
Merry Christmas!	merī kurisu-mas
Look after yourself. (take care)	o-daiji-ni

Also Available
QUICK AND EASY WAY TO LEARN HINDI
Quick
and
Easy
Way to
Learn
French
Vishakha Sharma